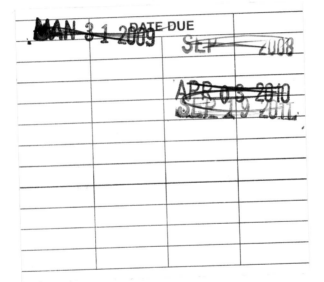

CLEVER RACCOONS

by Kristin L. Nelson

Pull Ahead Books

Lerner Publications Company • Minneapolis

To my son, Ethan—KLN

12/07
14.60

This book is available in two editions:
Library binding by Lerner Publications Company,
  a division of Lerner Publishing Group
Soft cover by First Avenue Editions,
  an imprint of Lerner Publishing Group
241 First Avenue North, Minneapolis, MN 55401 U.S.A.

Website address: www.lernerbooks.com

Words in *italic type* are explained in a glossary on page 30.

Library of Congress Cataloging-in-Publication Data

Nelson, Kristin (Kristin L.)
    Clever raccoons / by Kristin Nelson.
       p.   cm. — (Pull ahead books)
    Includes index.
    Summary: Simple text and photographs introduce the physical characteristics, behavior, and habitat of the raccoon.
    ISBN 0–8225–3763–X (lib. bdg. : alk. paper)
    ISBN 0–8225–3644–7 (pbk. : alk. paper)
    1. Raccoons—Juvenile literature. [1. Raccoons]
I. Title. II. Series.
QL737.C26 N448 2001
599.76'36—dc21   99-050405

Manufactured in the United States of America
 3 4 5 6 7 — JR — 07 06 05 04

This clever animal can live in many places.

It can even live in your backyard!
What animal is it?

This animal is a raccoon.

Most raccoons live in forests
and meadows.

They can live in cities
and near beaches, too.

How can raccoons live
in so many different places?

Raccoons live wherever they can
find food and a safe home.

Most raccoons live near water.

Raccoons are great swimmers.

Many raccoons make their homes inside old trees that are near water.

These cozy homes are called *dens.*

This raccoon put leaves on the bottom of its den.

Leaves make the den soft and warm.

Raccoons stay in their den
most of the day.

They look for food at night.

Animals that are active at night are *nocturnal*.

Are you nocturnal?

Raccoons look for many
kinds of food.

They eat fruit, nuts, and small
animals such as fish and mice.

Raccoons
are
omnivores.

Omnivores are animals that eat
both plants and other animals.

Raccoons use their front *paws*
to grab food.

They use
their sharp
teeth to
chew the
food.

Each of their four paws has five
fingers and five sharp claws.

A raccoon's
front paws
move like
your hands.

Raccoons are great climbers.

They use their claws to hold onto
the bark of trees.

Look out! Sometimes raccoons climb down trees head first.

What do you see around the eyes of this raccoon?

Raccoons have black fur
around their eyes.

The fur looks like a mask.

They have
black stripes
around their
tails.

This raccoon is squeezing
into its den.

Baby raccoons are born without masks or stripes.

They have gray, fuzzy fur.

Baby raccoons are called *kits.*

Kits are born with their eyes closed.

Raccoons are part of a group of animals called *mammals.*

Like all baby mammals, raccoon kits drink milk from their mother.

After about three weeks, the kits can open their eyes.

These kits are looking at the world around them.

After about ten weeks, kits start to follow their mother outside the den.

They learn to hunt for food.
They learn to climb trees.

When a kit is about one year old,
it is ready to live on its own.

Raccoons can live in many places.

They can eat many kinds of food.

Have you ever seen a clever
raccoon in your backyard?

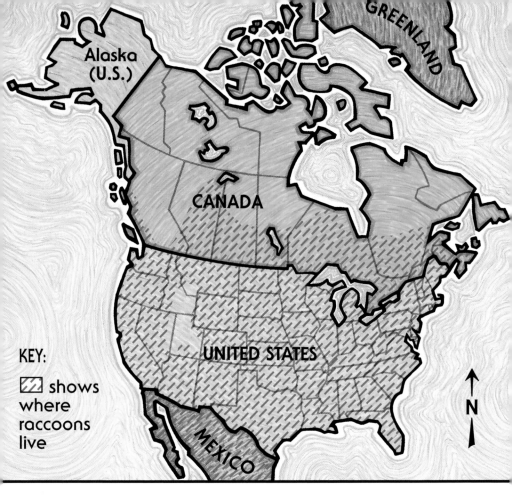

Find your state or province on this map.
Do raccoons live near you?

Parts of a Raccoon's Body

Glossary

dens: cozy animal homes

kits: baby raccoons

mammal: an animal that has fur or hair and drinks mother's milk when young. Some mammals are humans, bears, raccoons, and whales.

nocturnal: active at night

omnivores: animals that eat both plants and other animals

paw: the foot of a four-footed animal that has claws

Hunt and Find

- raccoons **eating** on pages 12–14

- raccoons **climbing** on pages 16–17, 21, 27

- raccoons in their **dens** on pages 8–9, 19, 23

- raccoon **kits** on pages 20–25

- where raccoons **live** on pages 3–8

- a raccoon's **paws** on pages 14–15

- raccoons **by water** on pages 6–7, 13, 24, 26

The publisher wishes to extend special thanks to our **series consultant,** Sharyn Fenwick. An elementary science-math specialist, Mrs. Fenwick was the recipient of the National Science Teachers Association 1991 Distinguished Teaching Award. In 1992, representing the state of Minnesota at the elementary level, she received the Presidential Award for Excellence in Math and Science Teaching.

About the Author

Kristin L. Nelson has fond childhood memories of watching raccoons near her family's wooded home in Minnesota. She looks forward to the day when her two-year-old son spots one of those curious creatures in their backyard. Kristin likes to read, sing jazz, walk, and bike. She lives in Savage, Minnesota, with her husband, Bob, and son, Ethan. This is her first book.

Photo Acknowledgments

The photographs in this book are reproduced through the courtesy of: © Rich Kirchner, front cover, pages 6, 18; © Alan and Sandy Carey, back cover, pages 4, 24, 27; © Anne Laird, pages 3, 31; © C. C. Lockwood/ Animals Animals, pages 5, 22; © Leonard Rue Enterprises/Leonard Lee Rue III, pages 7, 8, 19, 20, 21, 23, 25; © Visuals Unlimited: (John Sohlden) page 9, (Kurt Kamin) page 11, (Stephen J. Lang) page 12, (Joe McDonald) pages 13, 17, (W. J. Weber) page 15; © F. Gohier/The National Audubon Society Collection/Photo Researchers, Inc., page 10; © Beth Davidow, pages 14, 16; © Tom Browning, page 26.